Illustrated Biography for Children:

Thomas Edison

The Inventor Who Lit Up Our World

Visit our author page for more children's books
Amazon.com/author/88

By Nicole Damon

Thomas Edison: The Wizard of Menlo Park

Introduction: The Inventor Who Lit Up the World

Once upon a time, in a world where nights were dark and silent, there lived a man whose brilliant ideas would change everything. His name was Thomas Alva Edison, and he was destined to become one of the greatest inventors in history. People called him "The Wizard of Menlo Park," a magical place where his ideas came to life.

Thomas Edison was no ordinary man. With over 1,000 patents to his name, he was a master of invention. Imagine a world without music from speakers, movies at the cinema, or light at the flip of a switch. Hard to picture, isn't it? Well, we have Edison to thank for all of these and more!

He is best known for inventing the electric light bulb, a glowing orb that banished darkness and brought light to homes, streets, and cities around the world. But that's not all! He also created the phonograph, a marvelous machine that captured sound and played it back, allowing people to listen to music and voices as if by magic.

Edison's inventions didn't stop there. He was a tireless tinkerer, always experimenting, always dreaming up new ideas. From motion picture cameras to batteries, his creations have shaped the world we live in today.

The Young Inventor

Thomas Edison was not the kind of person who could sit still. Even as a young boy, he was always tinkering and thinking, his mind buzzing with ideas. By the time he was a teenager, he had already started to turn some of those ideas into inventions!

One of his first jobs was as a telegraph operator. This was a very important job back then, as the telegraph was the fastest way to send messages over long distances. Edison was fascinated by this technology, and he spent a lot of his free time experimenting with it. He even invented a machine to make telegraphy faster and easier!

But Edison's big moment came when he created his very first invention: the electric vote recorder. This clever device was meant to speed up the voting process in government. With just the push of a button, lawmakers could vote 'yes' or 'no,' and the machine would record their votes instantly.

Unfortunately, the politicians didn't want voting to be faster—they liked having time to change each other's minds! So, Edison's invention wasn't used, but he wasn't discouraged. He had caught the inventing bug, and there was no turning back.

Edison knew that if he wanted to be a full-time inventor, he needed a place where he could work on his ideas day and night. So, he packed up his tools and moved to Menlo Park, New Jersey. There, he set up his very own invention factory—a large laboratory where he and a team of brilliant scientists and engineers could experiment and create new inventions. It was the first research and development laboratory of its kind, and it was where Edison would invent some of his greatest creations.

Menlo Park was like a playground for Edison's imagination. It was filled with all sorts of gadgets, gizmos, and materials that he could use to bring his ideas to life. And bring them to life he did! The invention factory was always buzzing with activity, and it wasn't long before Edison's genius began to light up the world in ways no one had ever seen before.

So, with his lab set up and his mind racing with ideas, Edison was ready to embark on a journey of invention that would make him the Wizard of Menlo Park. But little did he know, his brightest idea was yet to come...

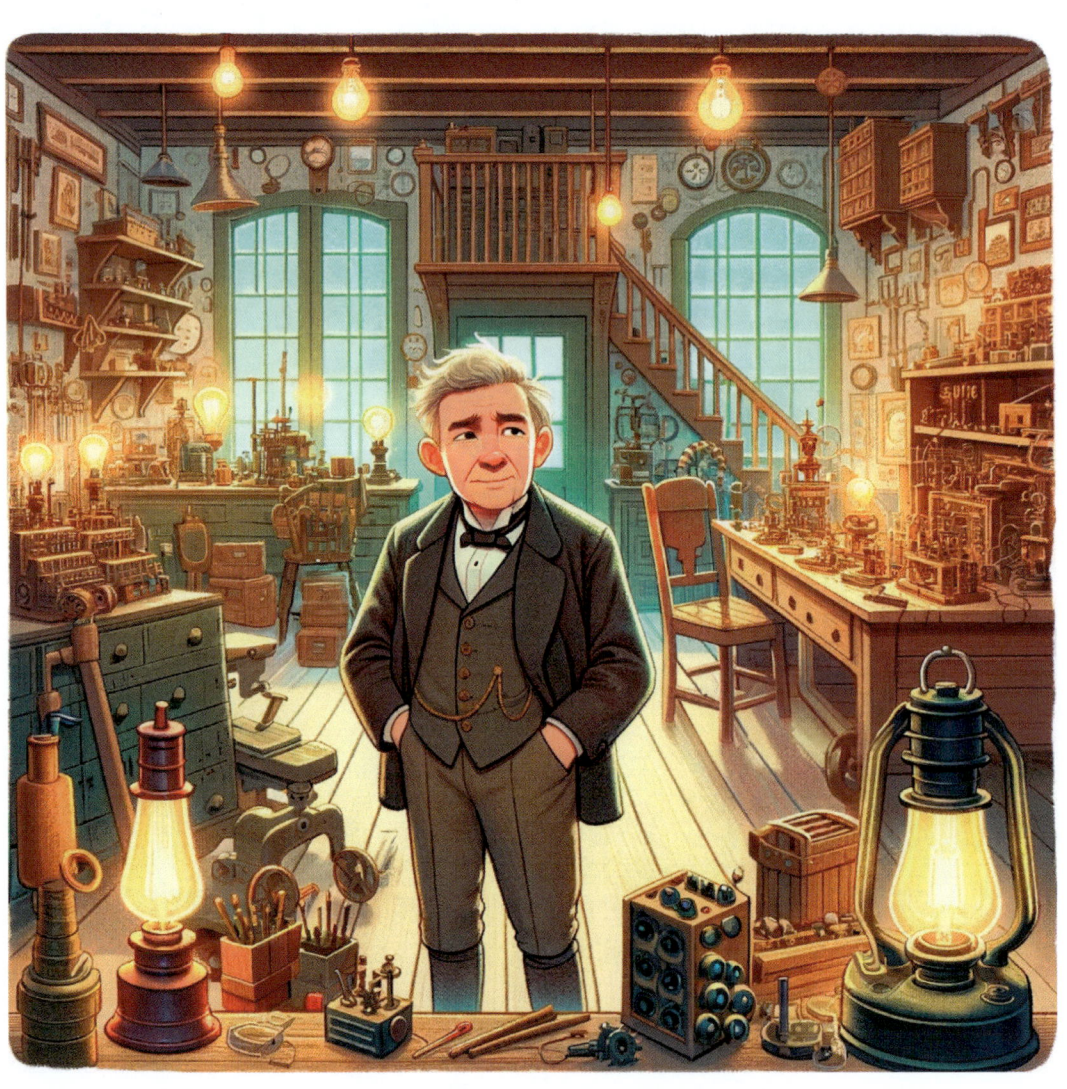

The Invention of the Phonograph

In the bustling laboratory of Menlo Park, amidst the clinking of tools and the hum of machinery, Thomas Edison was about to make a discovery that would astonish the world. It was a discovery that happened almost by accident, a stroke of genius that would give birth to a magical machine: the phonograph.

Edison was working on a completely different invention—a machine to record telegraph messages—when he noticed something curious. As the machine's stylus moved over the paper, it made a sound that resembled human speech. This unexpected observation sparked an idea in Edison's mind. What if he could create a machine that could record and play back not just dots and dashes, but actual sounds, even music and voices?

He swapped the paper for a metal cylinder wrapped in shiny tin foil, and instead of a stylus, he used a special needle that could both capture and play back sounds. After many trials and adjustments, the phonograph was born. When Edison first demonstrated the phonograph, people were amazed. They couldn't believe their ears!

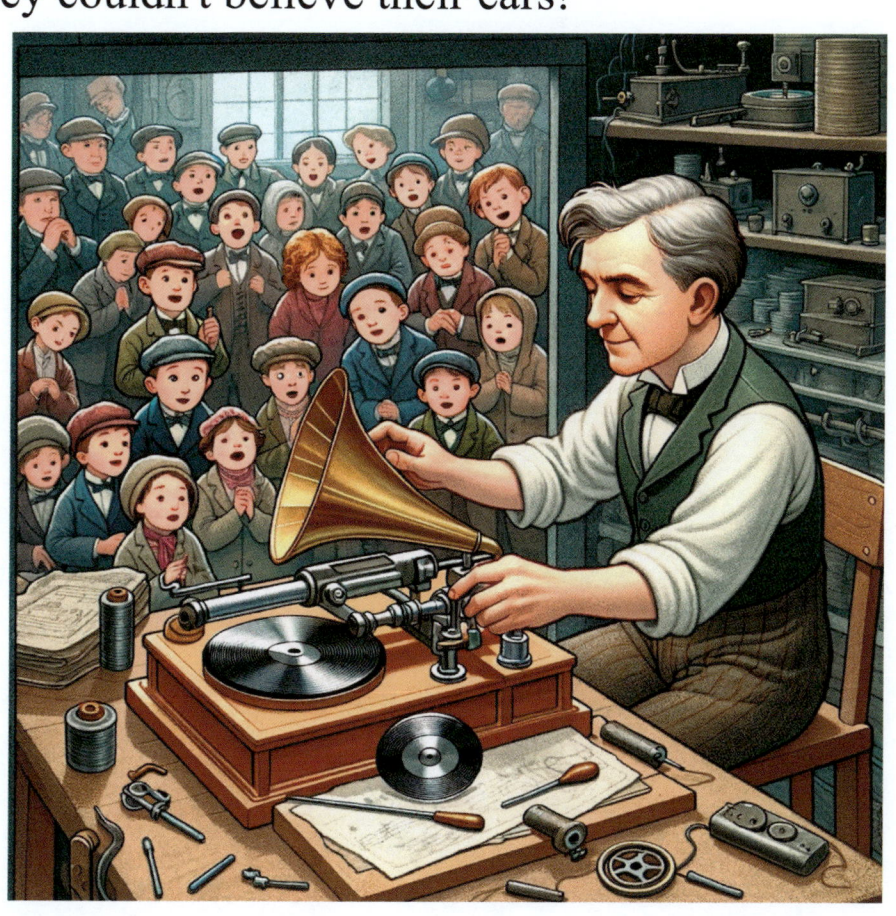

The machine, which Edison playfully called the "talking machine," could record someone's voice and then play it back, clear as day. It was like magic! The phonograph quickly became a sensation. People flocked to hear this incredible device that could capture and reproduce sound.

The phonograph changed entertainment forever. For the first time in history, music could be recorded and played back, allowing people to enjoy their favorite tunes anytime they wished. Families gathered around the phonograph to listen to music, stories, and even the voices of famous people. The invention paved the way for record players, cassette tapes, CDs, and all the ways we listen to music today.

Edison's phonograph was more than just an invention; it was a window to a new world of sound. It allowed people to preserve their voices and memories, to share music and laughter across time and space. The phonograph was a true marvel of its time, and it all started with a curious observation in Thomas Edison's lively laboratory.

Lighting Up the World

After the success of the phonograph, Thomas Edison was ready for his next big challenge. He wanted to tackle a problem that had puzzled scientists for years: how to create a practical electric light bulb. Back then, people used candles, gas lamps, and oil lamps to light their homes, which were smoky, smelly, and sometimes dangerous. Edison dreamed of a safer, cleaner, and brighter way to light up the world.

Edison knew this wouldn't be easy. Many inventors had tried and failed to make a reliable electric light bulb. But Edison was determined. He gathered a team of brilliant minds at his Menlo Park laboratory and set to work. They experimented with different materials for the filament—the part of the bulb that glows when it gets hot. They tried platinum, carbon, and even human hair!

Finally, after countless experiments, Edison and his team found the perfect material: a carbonized cotton thread. When they sent electricity through it, the filament glowed with a bright, steady light. It was a moment of triumph! On October 21, 1879, Edison's team lit up the first successful electric light bulb. It burned for a remarkable 13 and a half hours, proving that electric lighting was no longer just a dream.

The invention of the light bulb was a turning point in history. Edison went on to develop a whole system for generating and distributing electricity, so that electric light could reach homes and streets everywhere. Cities began to glow with the warm light of electric lamps. Nighttime became brighter and safer, and people's lives changed in countless ways.

With electric lighting, factories could stay open longer, and workers had better working conditions. Shops and theaters stayed open after dark, creating a bustling nightlife. Homes were brighter and cozier, and reading became easier on the eyes. The light bulb turned into a symbol of progress and new ideas, shining a light on a brand-new time in history.

Thanks to Edison and his team, the world was no longer a dark place when the sun went down. The invention of the light bulb was like a sunrise that spread across the globe, bringing light and warmth to everyone's lives. Edison truly lived up to his nickname, the "Wizard of Menlo Park," by casting a spell of light that still shines brightly today.

The Power of Electricity

Thomas Edison's groundbreaking invention of the light bulb was a brilliant achievement, but he knew that for it to truly light up the world, he needed a way to get electricity to people's homes and businesses. This was a big challenge, but Edison was up for it. He set out to create a system for generating and distributing electricity, a task that would change the world forever.

Edison built the first power station in New York City, called the Pearl Street Station. It was like a giant powerhouse, filled with huge machines called dynamos that generated electricity. From this station, electricity traveled through wires to light up homes and businesses in the surrounding area. It was the beginning of the electric age, and people were amazed to see their streets and buildings come alive with electric light.

But there was a problem. Edison's system used direct current (DC) electricity, which couldn't travel very far without losing power. This meant that power stations had to be built close to where the electricity was used, which wasn't very practical for lighting up whole cities.

Enter Nikola Tesla, a brilliant inventor with a different idea. Tesla believed that alternating current (AC) electricity was the solution. AC could travel long distances without losing power, making it possible to have fewer, larger power stations that could serve wider areas.

This difference in opinion sparked the "War of Currents" between Edison and Tesla. It was a battle of ideas, with Edison pushing for DC and Tesla advocating for AC. The war was heated, with both sides trying to prove that their system was better and safer.

In the end, AC won out. Tesla's ideas were adopted, and today, AC electricity powers our homes and cities. But Edison's work was not in vain. His pioneering efforts in creating the first power station and his tireless work in developing electric light laid the foundation for the modern electric world.

The establishment of the Pearl Street Station was a milestone in history. It marked the beginning of a new era, where electricity would become a central part of people's lives. Thanks to Edison's vision and determination, the power of electricity was harnessed, and the world was forever transformed.

The Legacy of an Inventor

Thomas Edison's journey as an inventor didn't stop with the light bulb or the power station. His curious mind was always on the move, dreaming up new inventions that would continue to change the world. Among these were the motion picture camera and alkaline batteries, innovations that still impact our lives today.

Edison's motion picture camera, called the Kinetograph, was one of the first devices to capture moving images on film. This invention opened the door to the world of cinema, allowing people to watch stories come to life on the big screen. Imagine a world without movies to enjoy on a rainy afternoon or without your favorite cartoons—thanks to Edison, we don't have to!

Then there were his alkaline batteries, a type of battery that lasts much longer than the ones that were available at the time. These batteries have been used in everything from flashlights to toys, making them an essential part of our everyday lives.

But Edison's influence went beyond just his inventions. He was also a savvy business leader. He founded several companies to manufacture and sell his inventions, the most famous of which was General Electric. Today, General Electric is one of the largest and most diverse companies in the world, involved in everything from energy to healthcare.

Edison's impact on the modern world is immeasurable. His inventions laid the groundwork for many of the technologies we take for granted today. Electric lights, movies, recorded music, batteries—these are just a few of the things that shape our daily lives, all thanks to Edison's genius.

As we reflect on Edison's legacy, it's clear that he was more than just an inventor. He was a visionary who saw the potential of electricity and harnessed it to light up our world. His tireless work ethic and relentless curiosity are an inspiration to us all.

Edison believed that the secret to genius was not just having great ideas, but putting in a lot of hard work to make them a reality. He showed us that with dedication and effort, even the most amazing inventions can come to life.

His life and achievements are a testament to the power of hard work and imagination. So, the next time you flip a light switch, watch a movie, or use a battery-powered device, remember Thomas Edison—the Wizard of Menlo Park who, with a spark of genius and a lot of hard work, helped create the world we live in today.

Visit our author page for more children's books,
and remember to follow us for updates on new releases,
including illustrated storybooks, biographies,
fun-fact books, coloring books for kids, and more:

www.amazon.com/author/88

Printed in Great Britain
by Amazon